I0391160

Coloring Our Traditions

Native American Themed Coloring Book

By: Weeya Michelle Smith

ISBN-13: 978-1540598646

ISBN-10: 1540598640

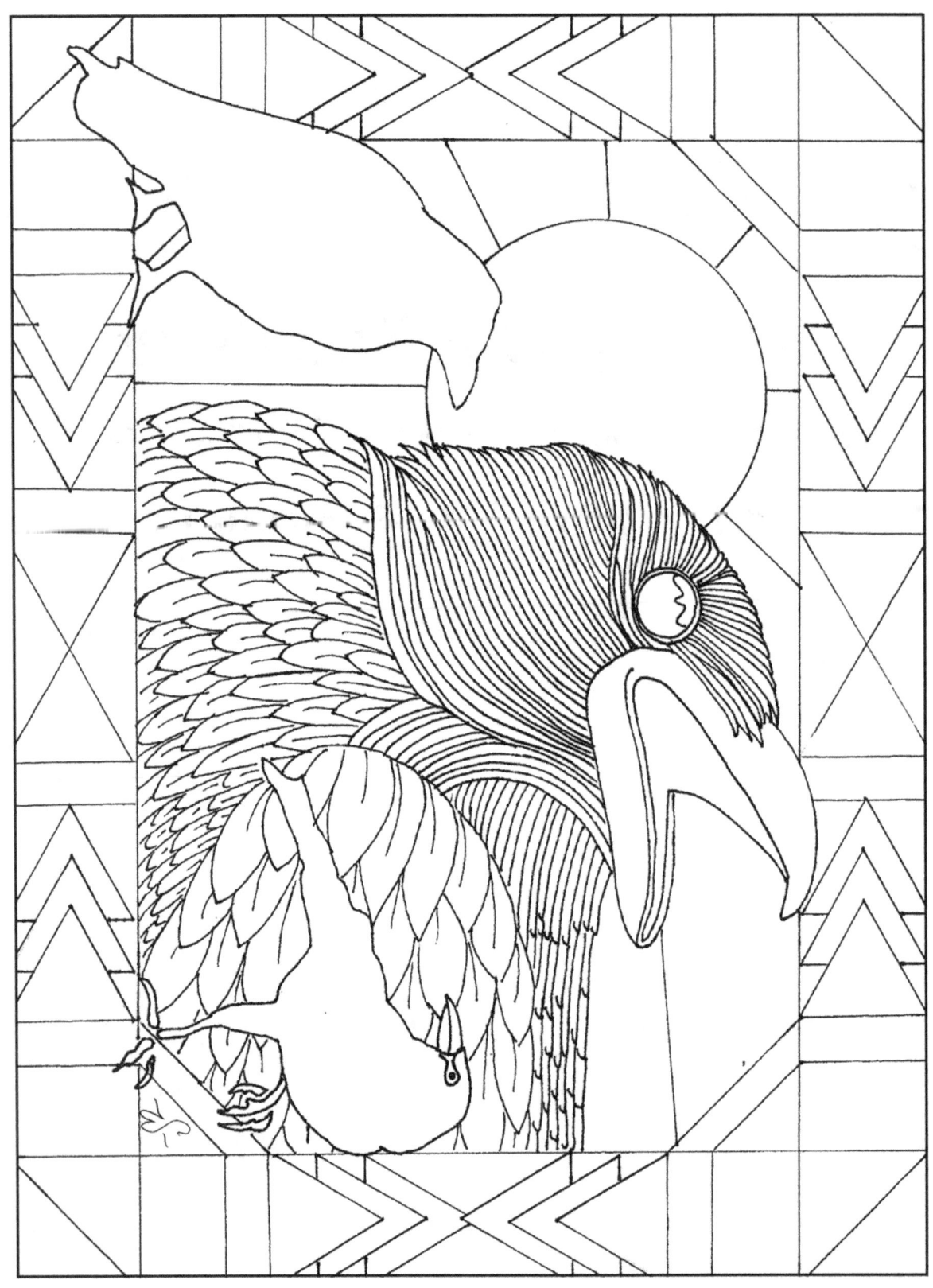

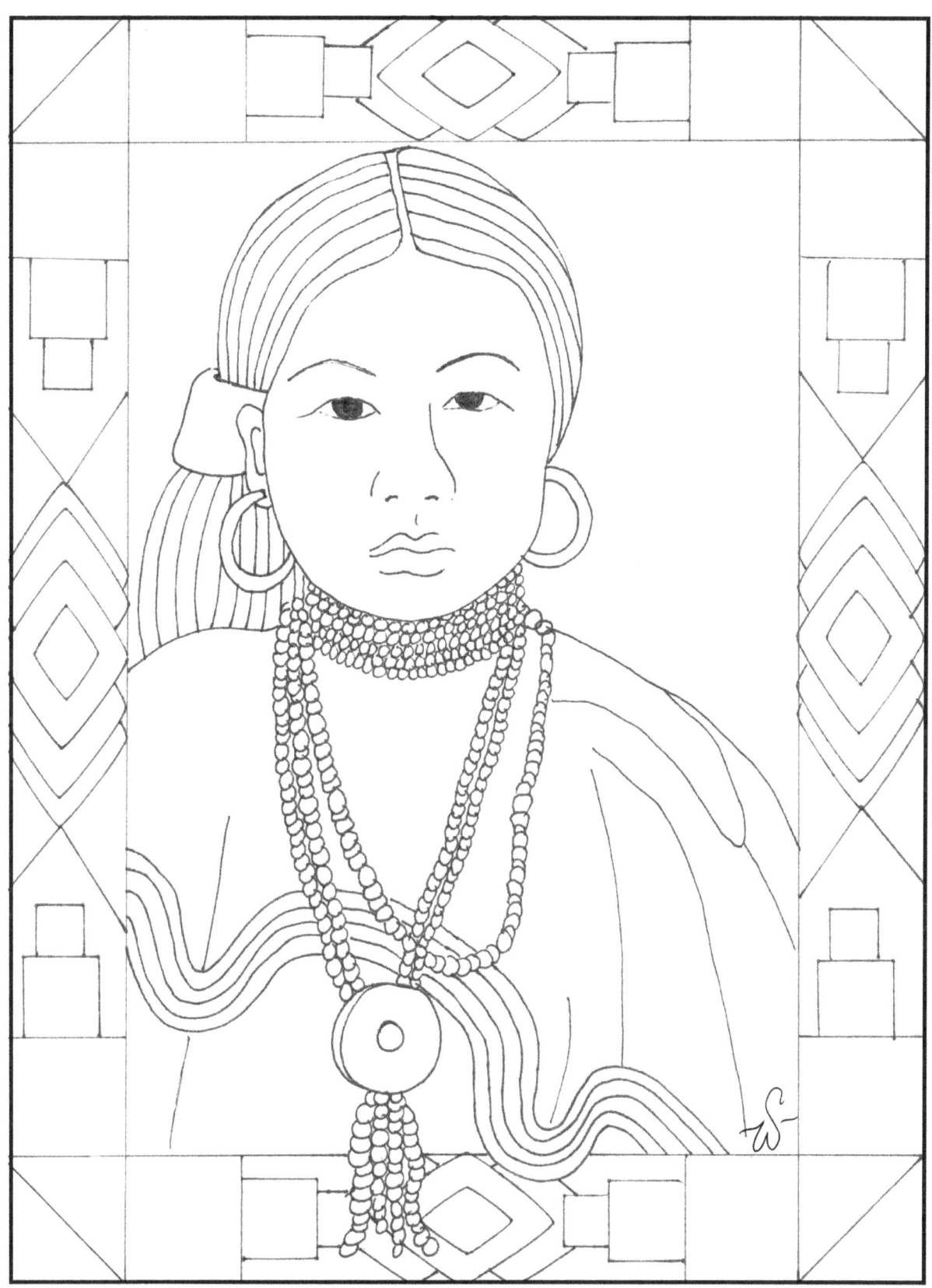

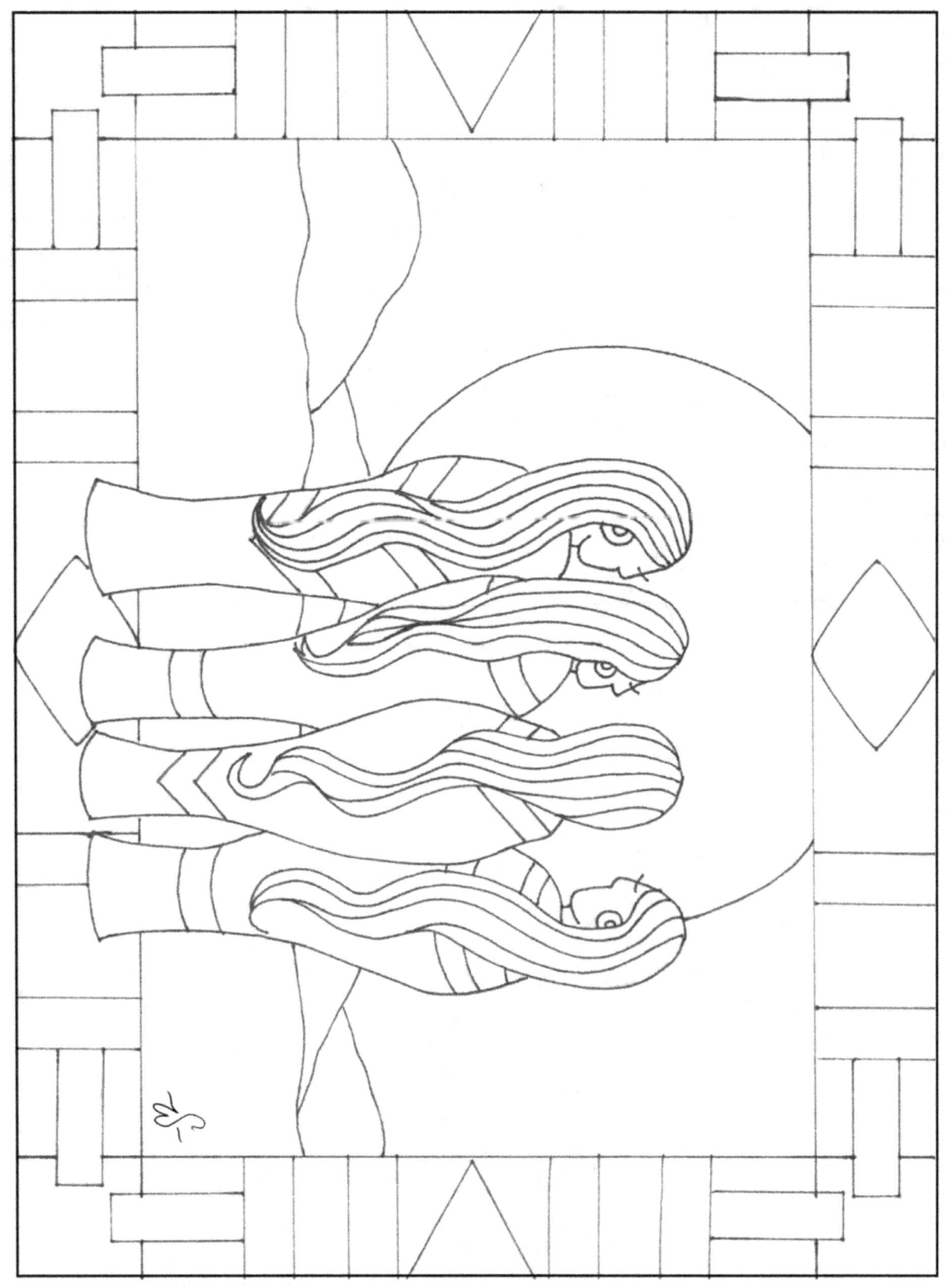

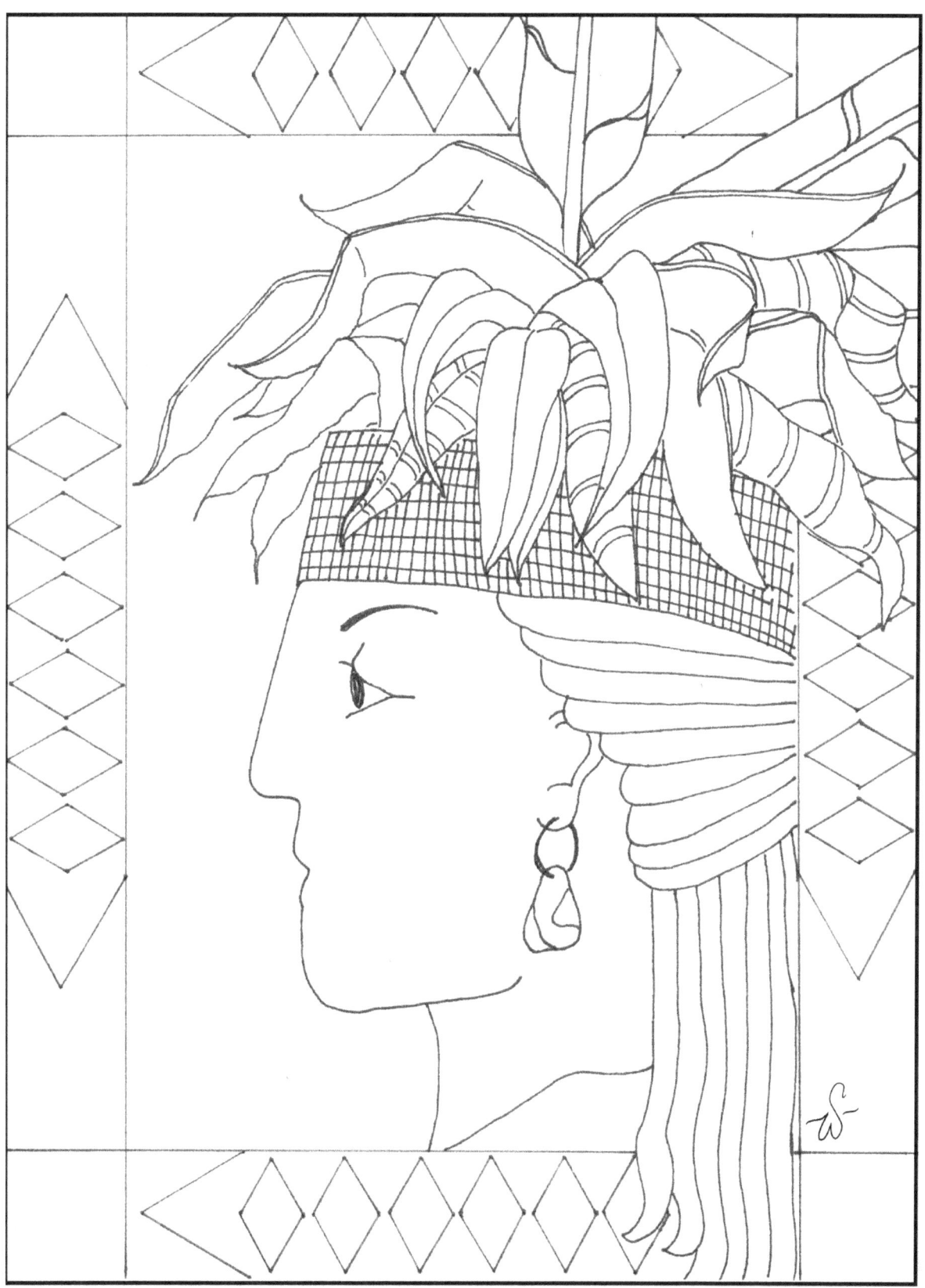

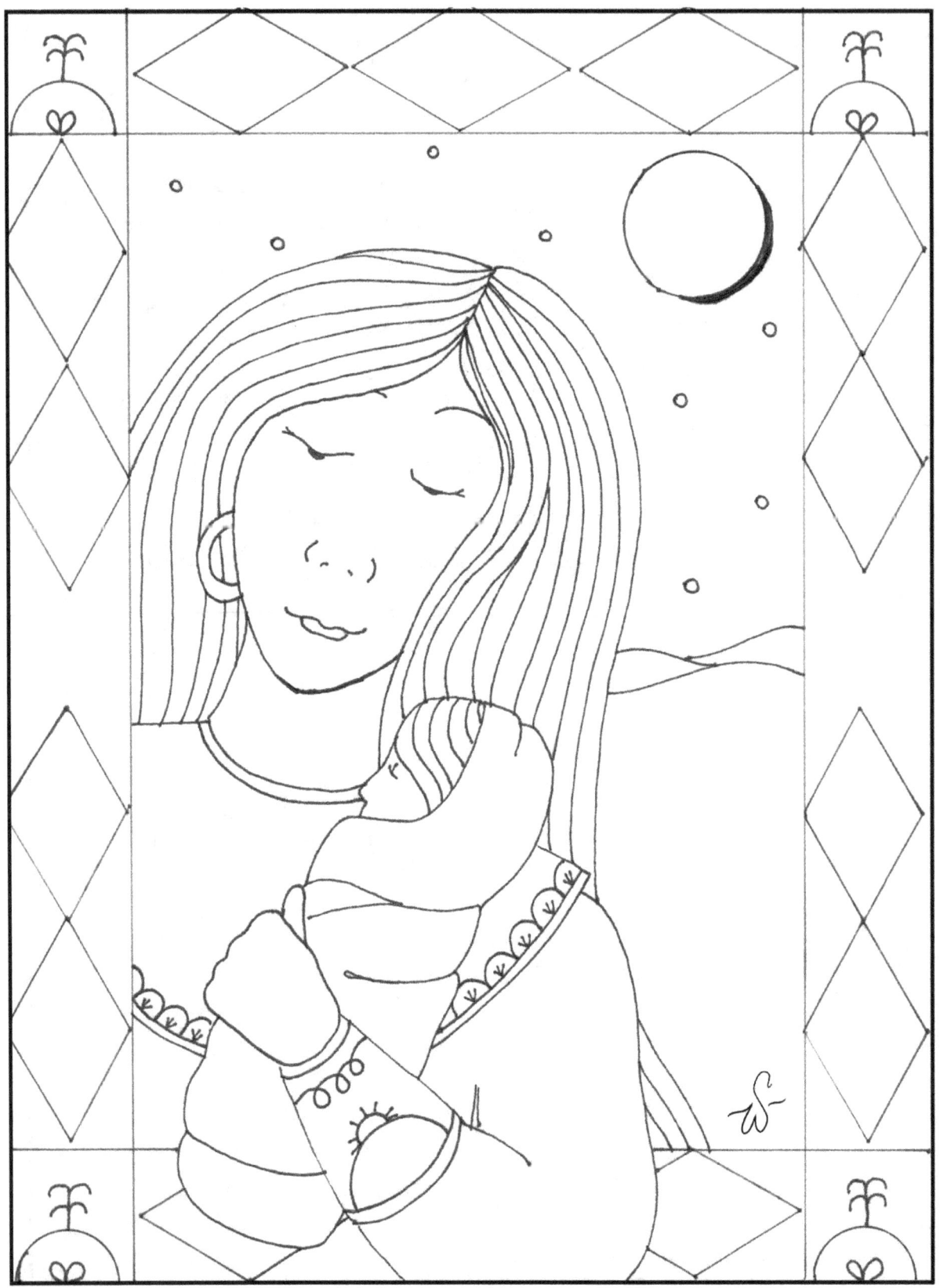

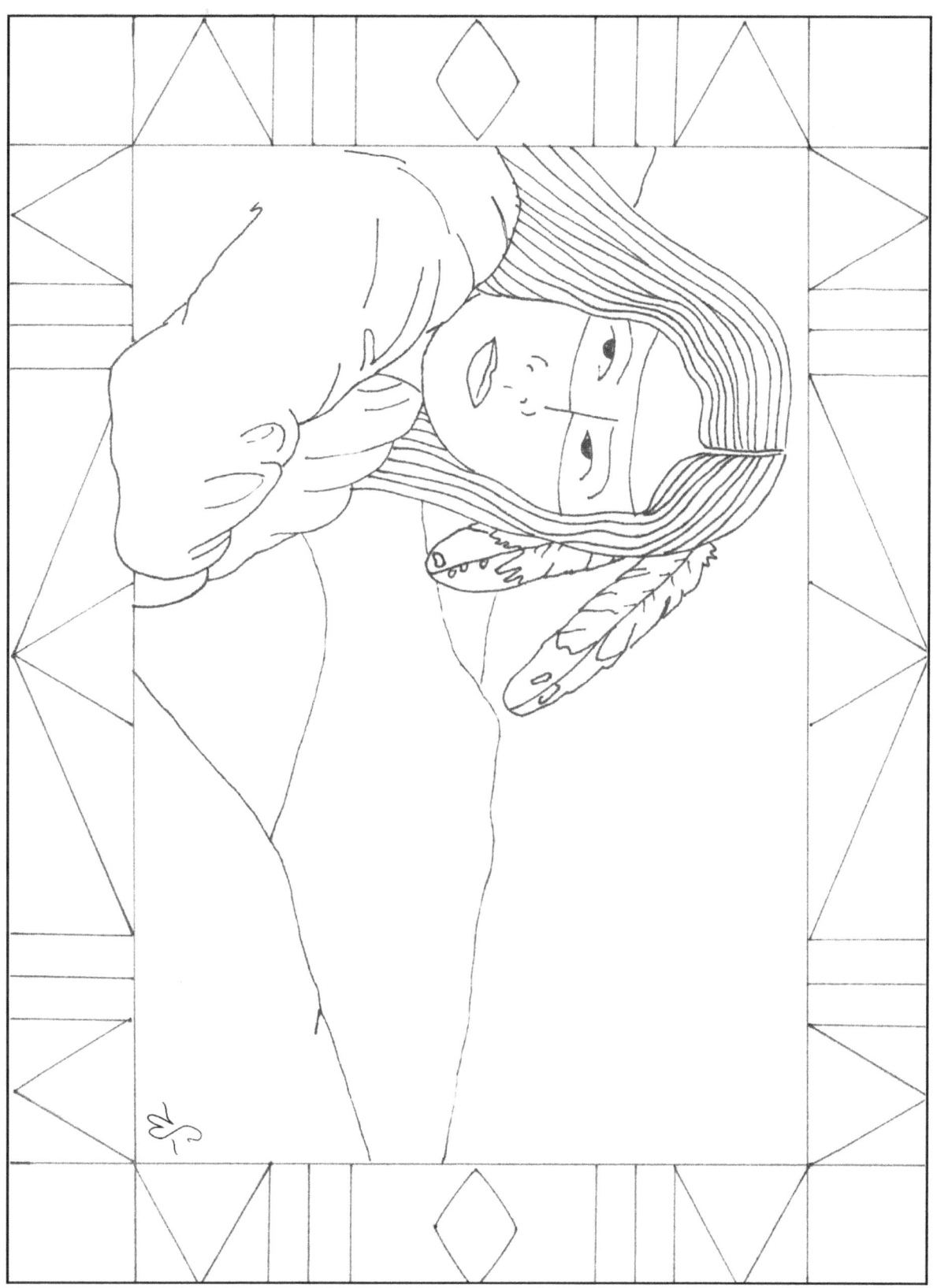

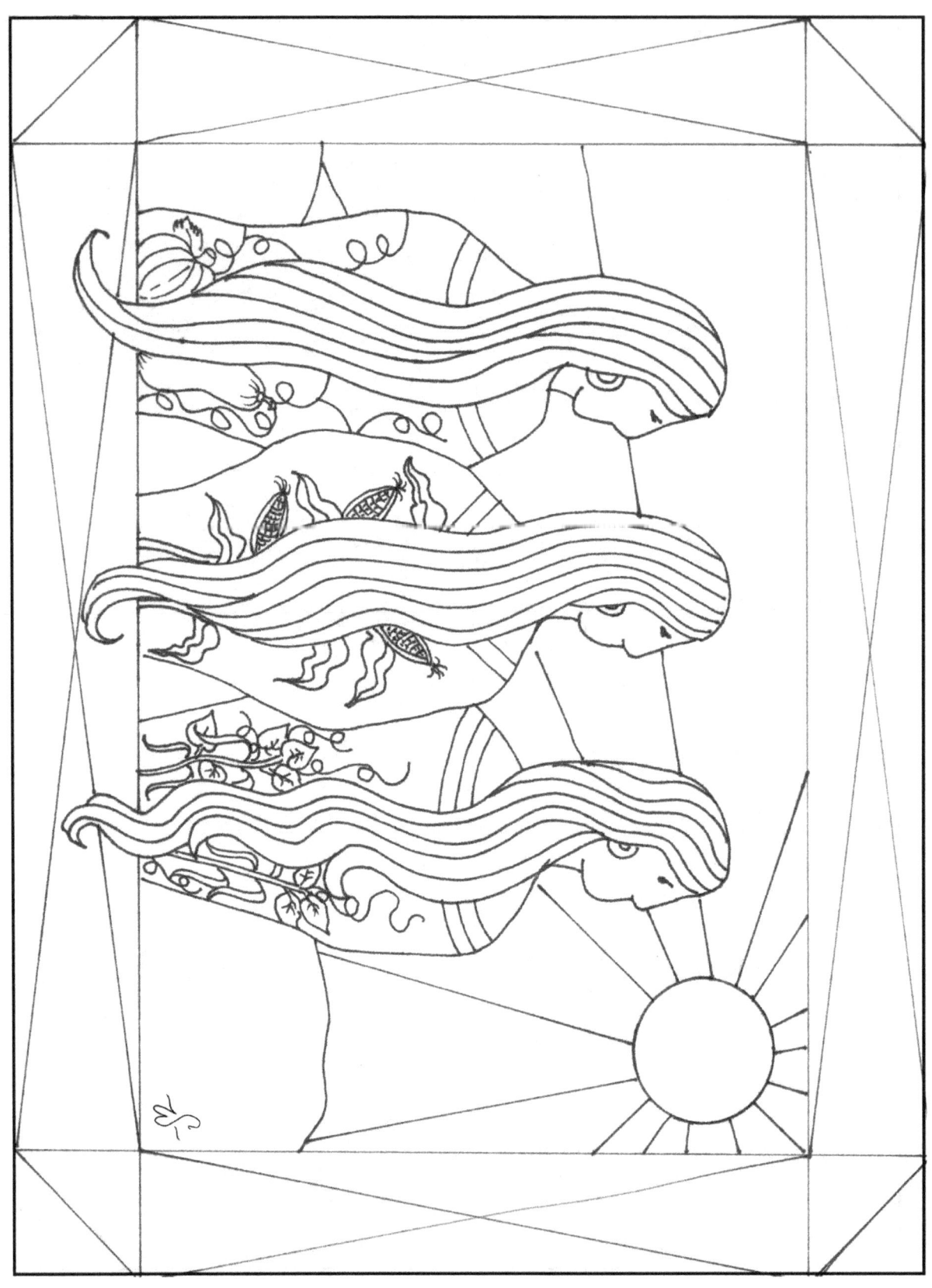

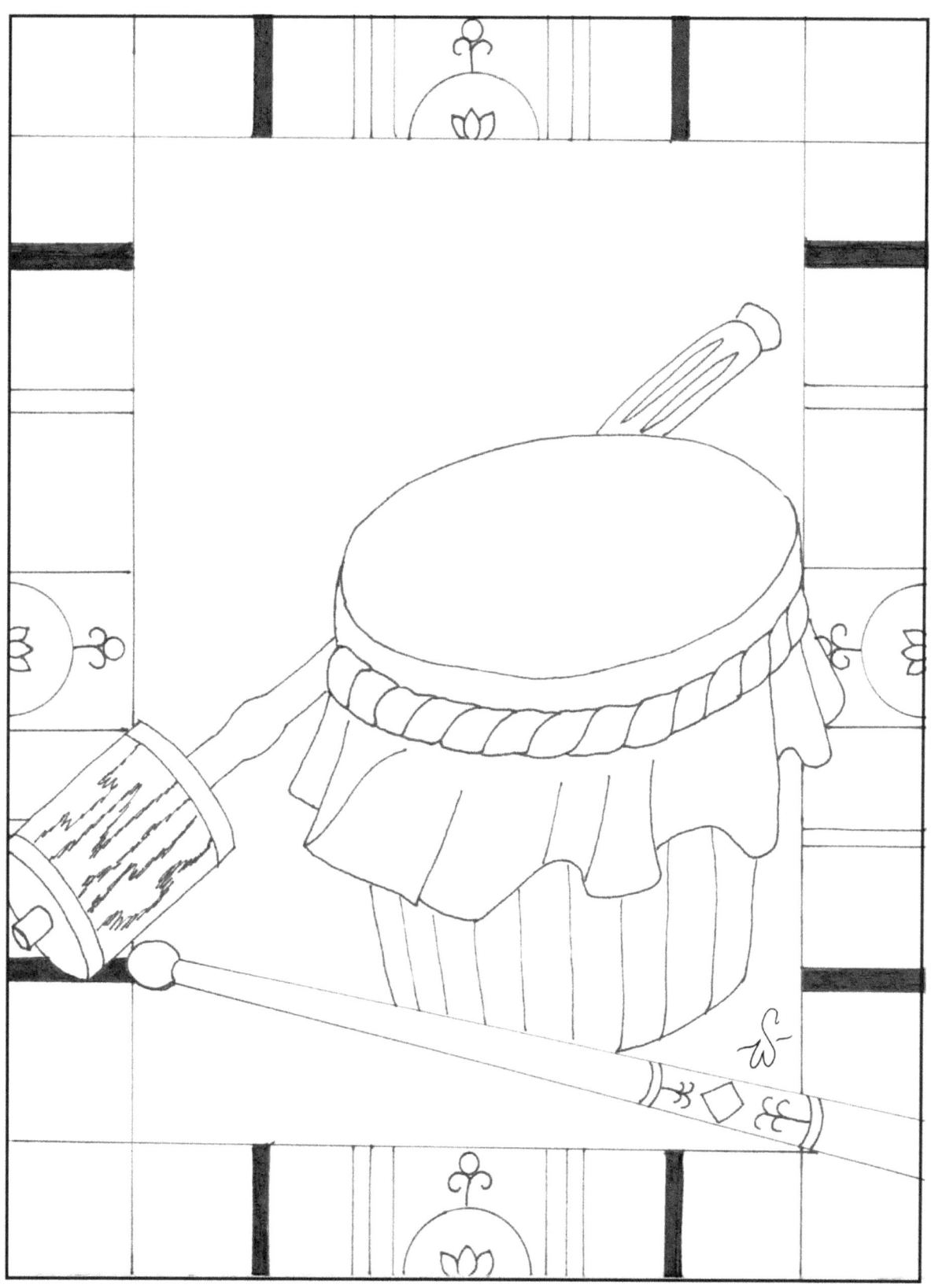

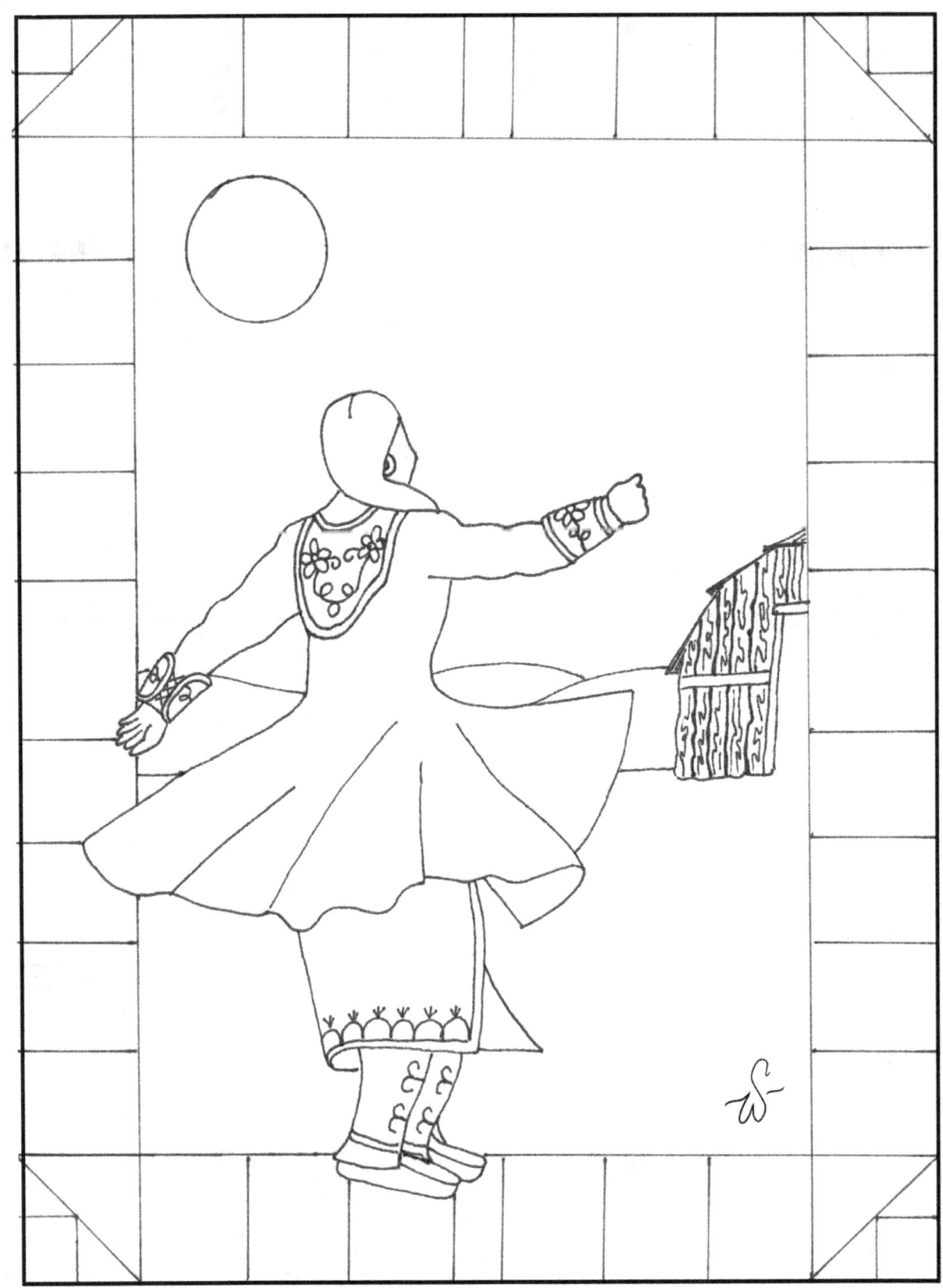

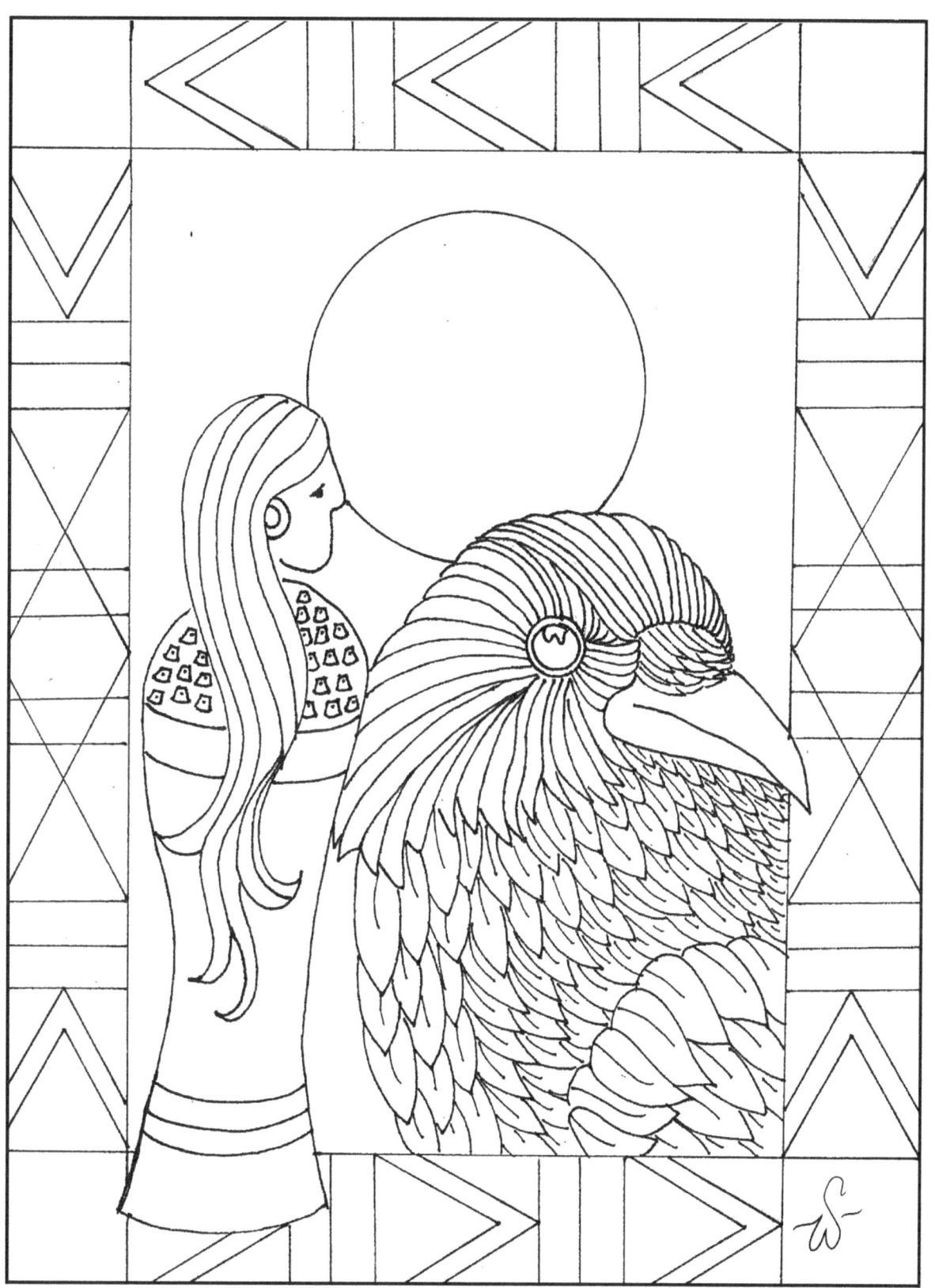

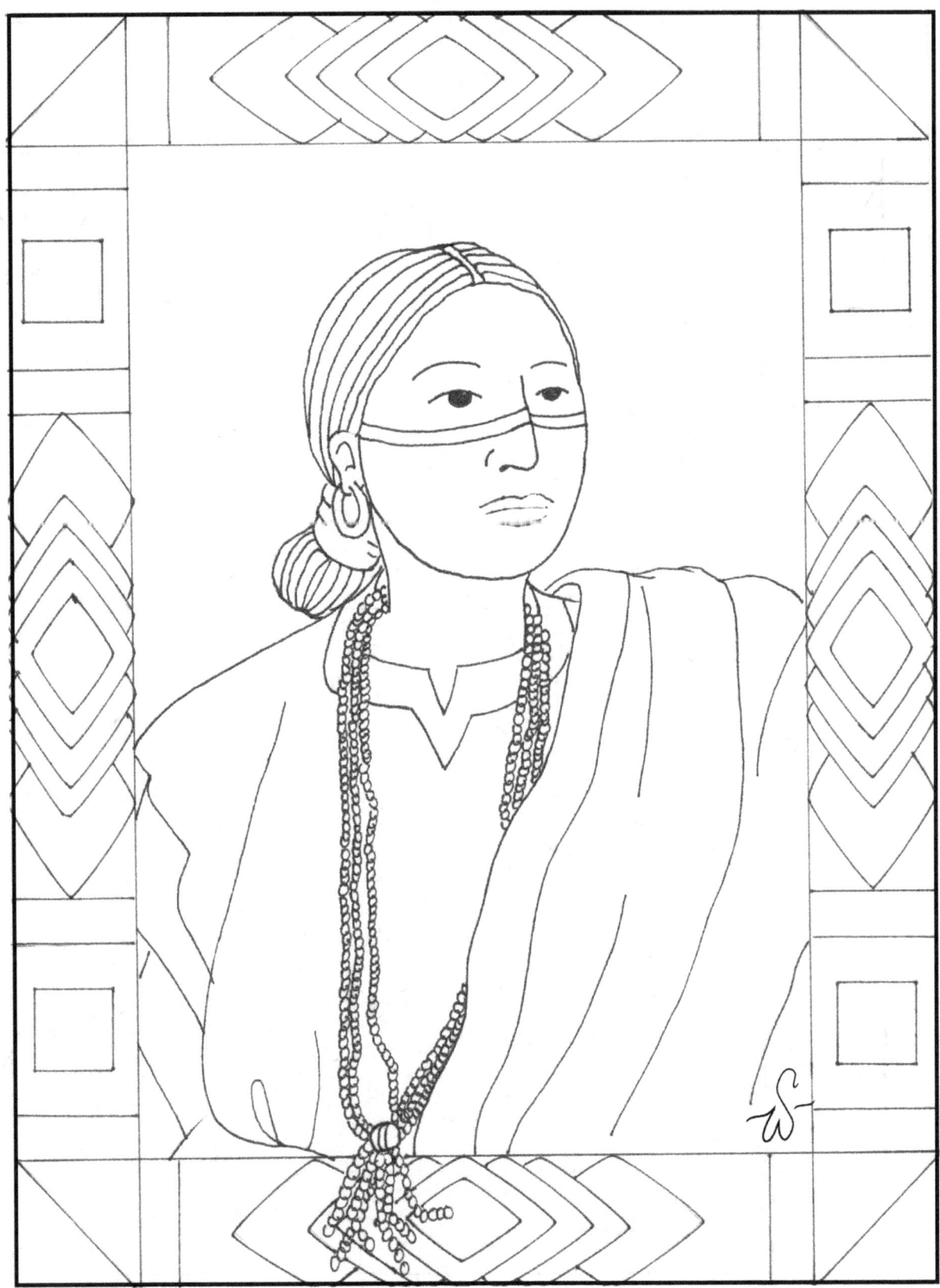

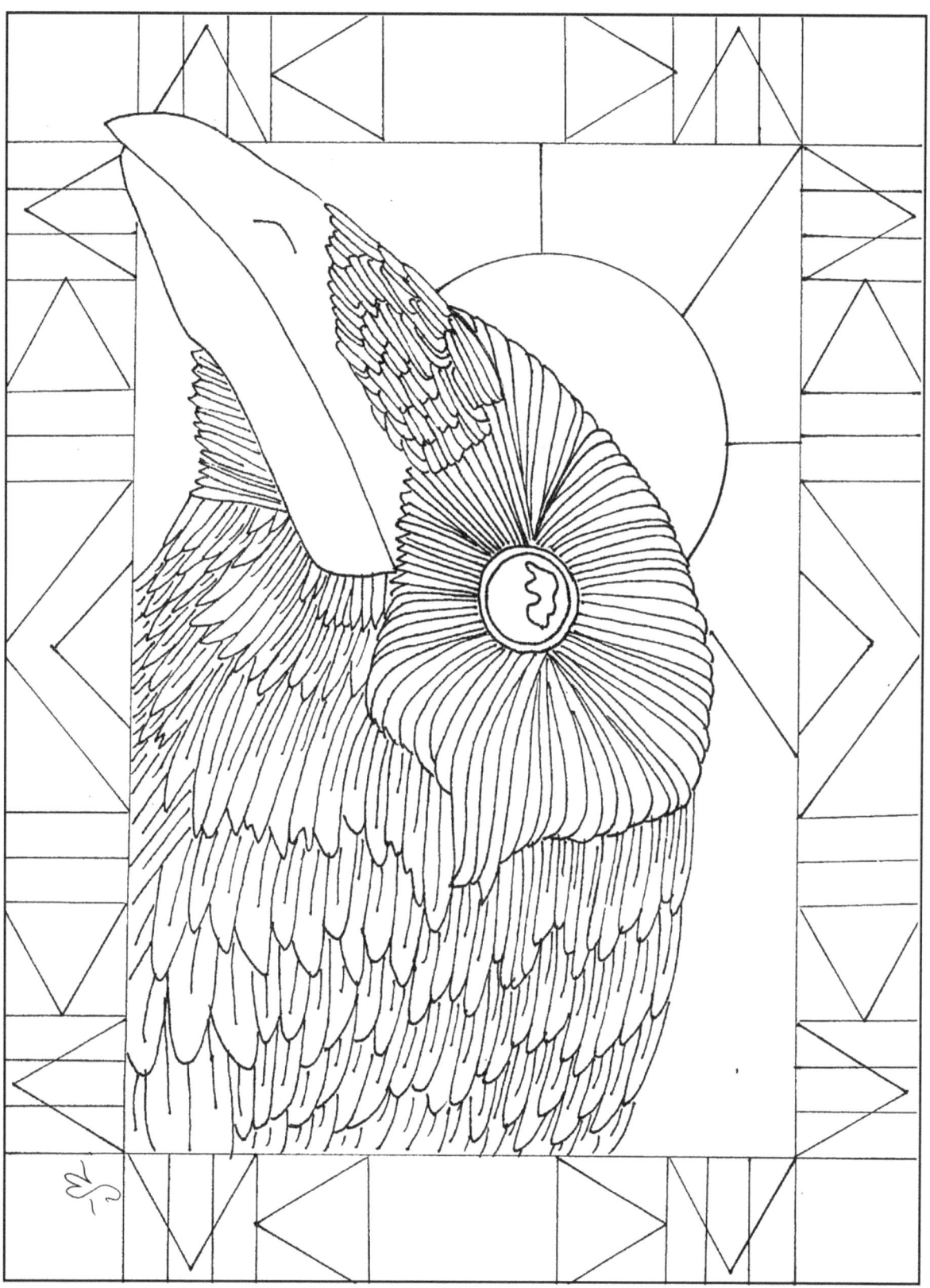

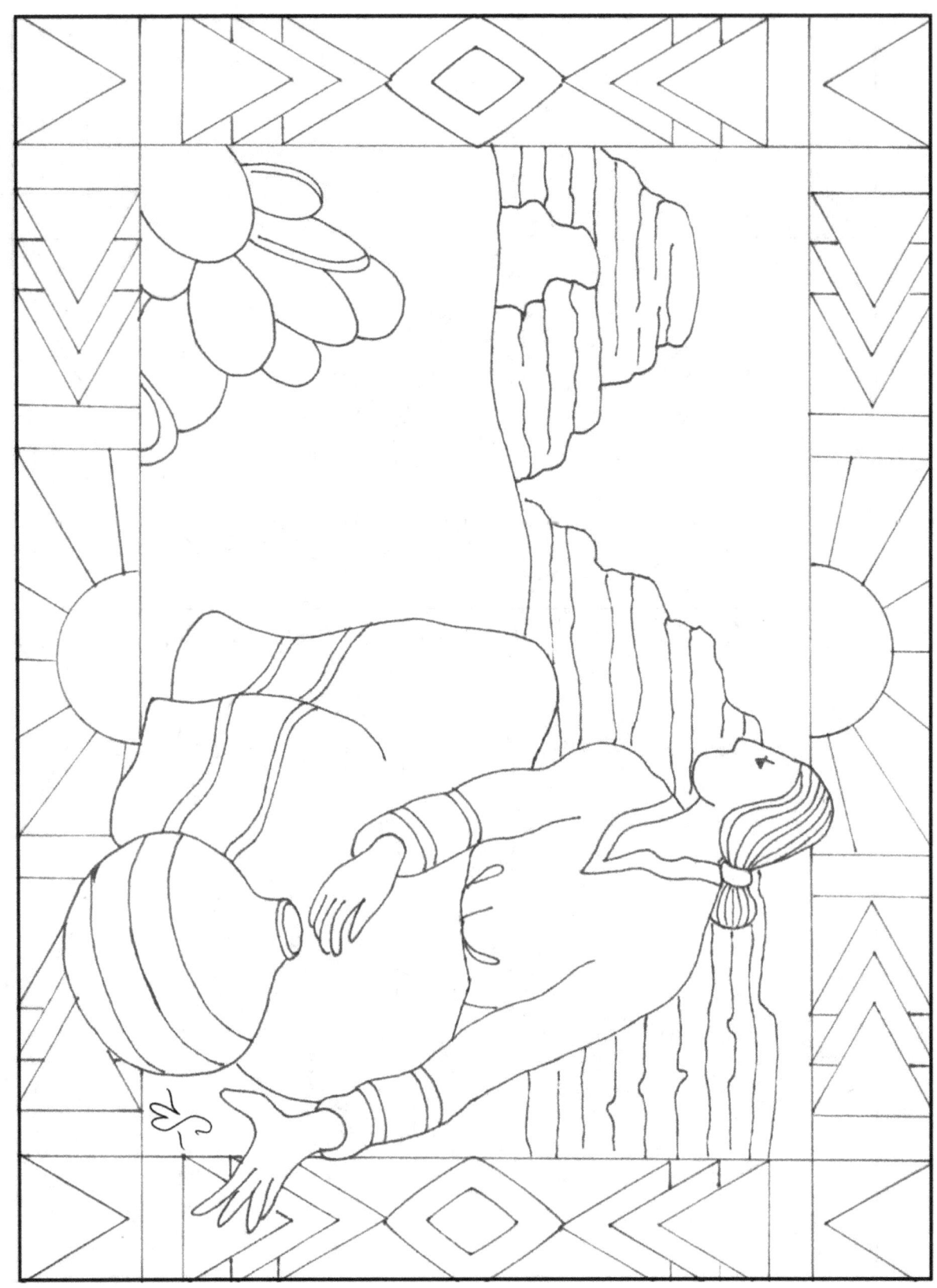

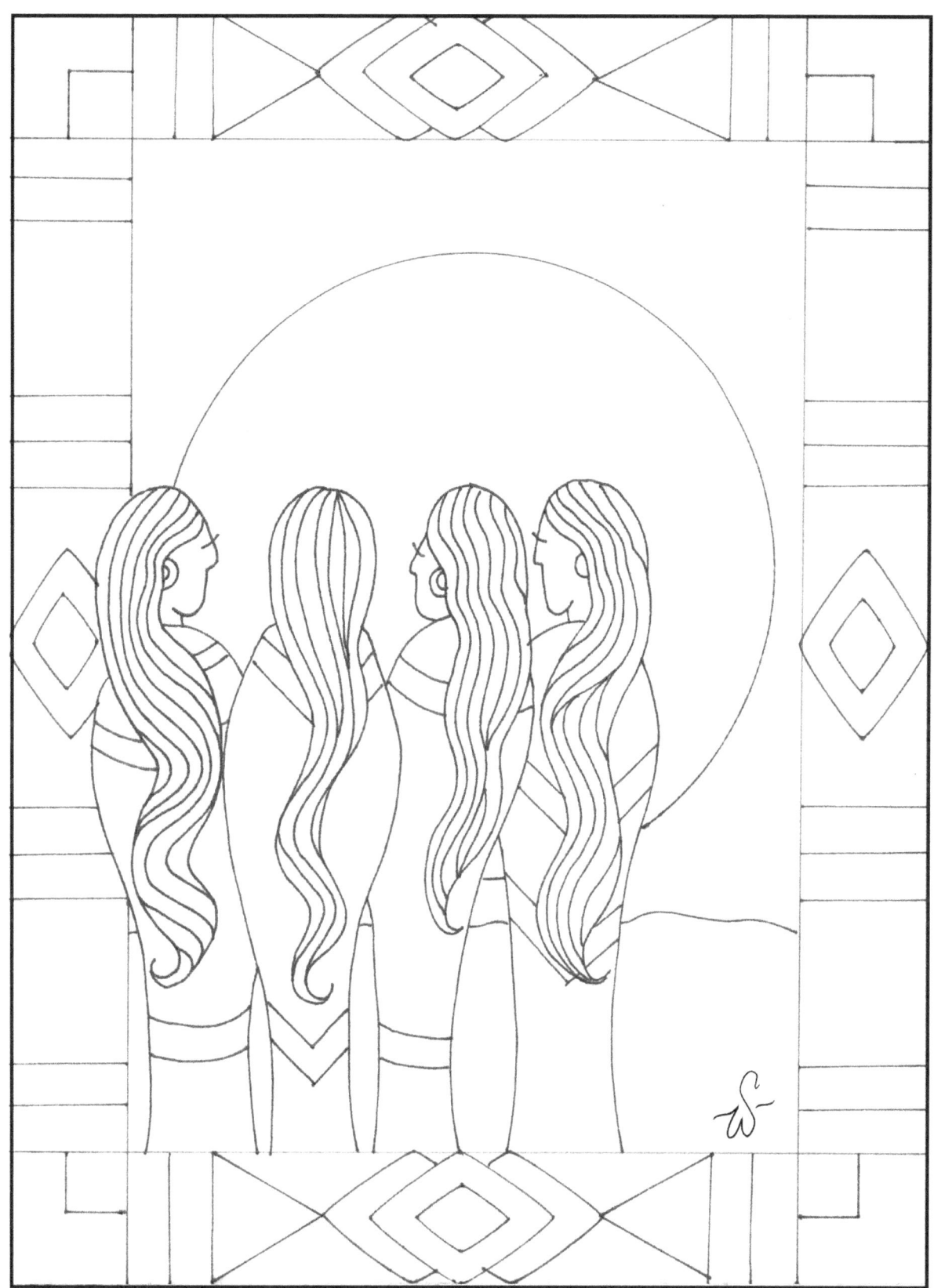

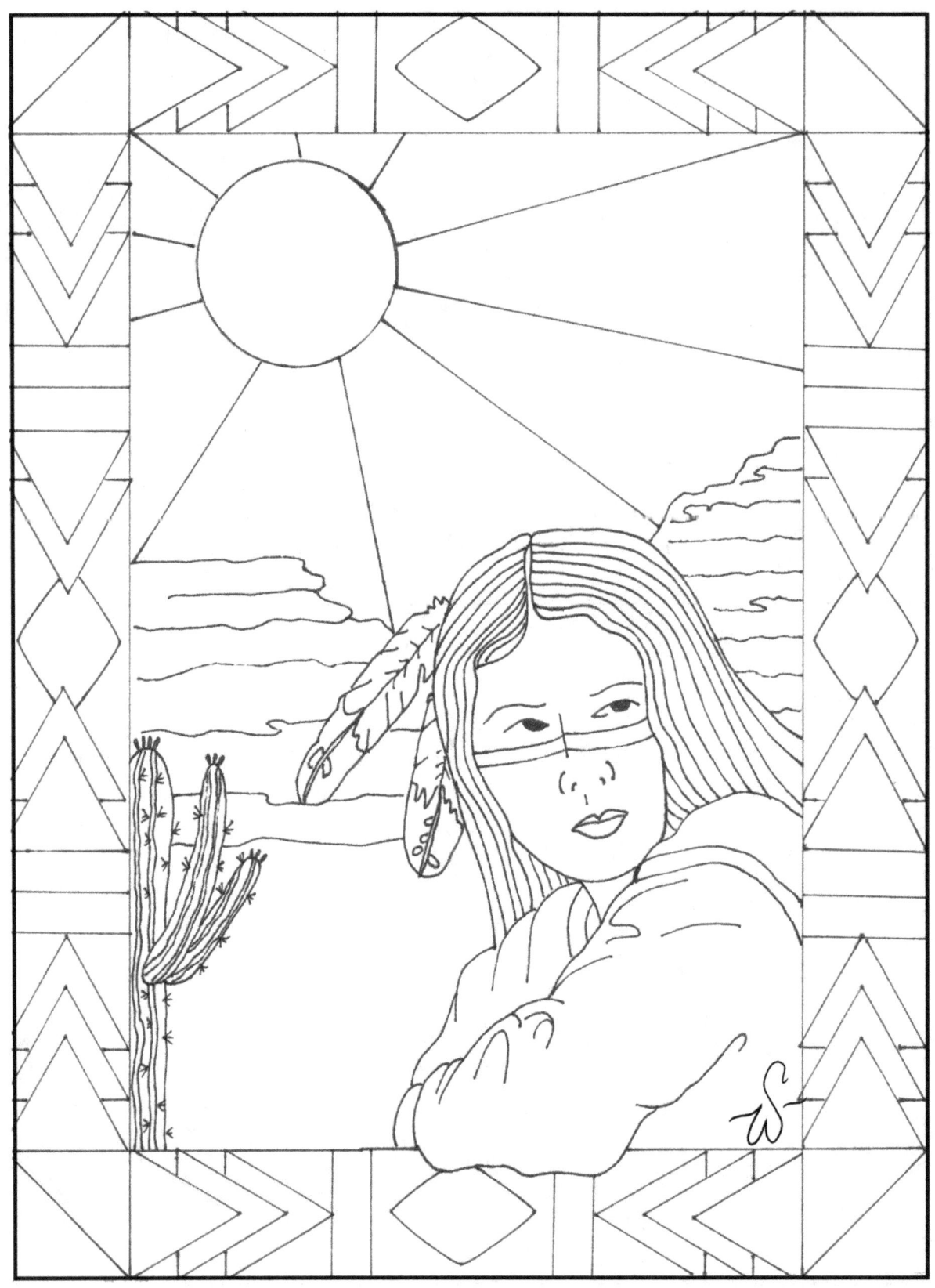

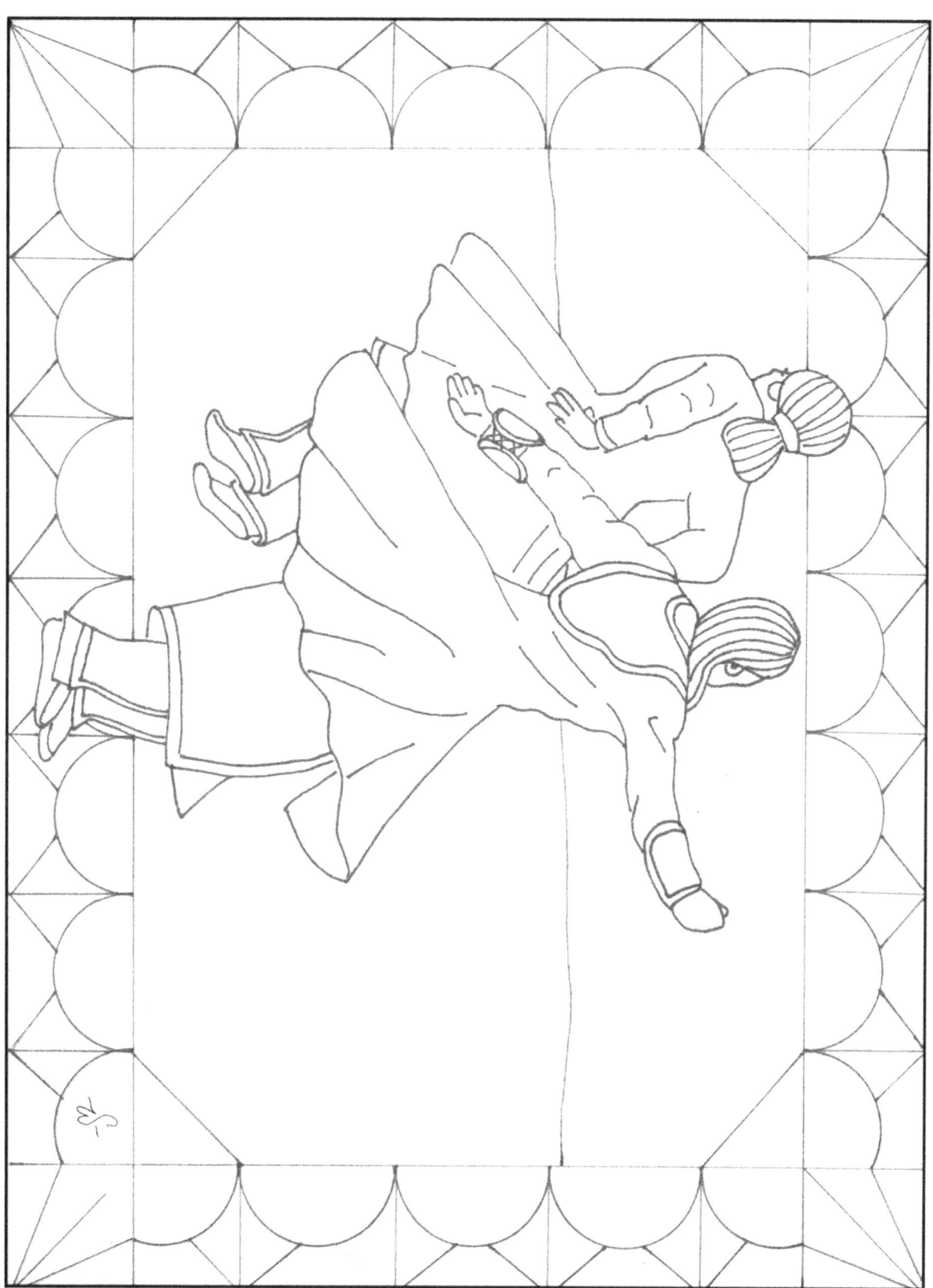

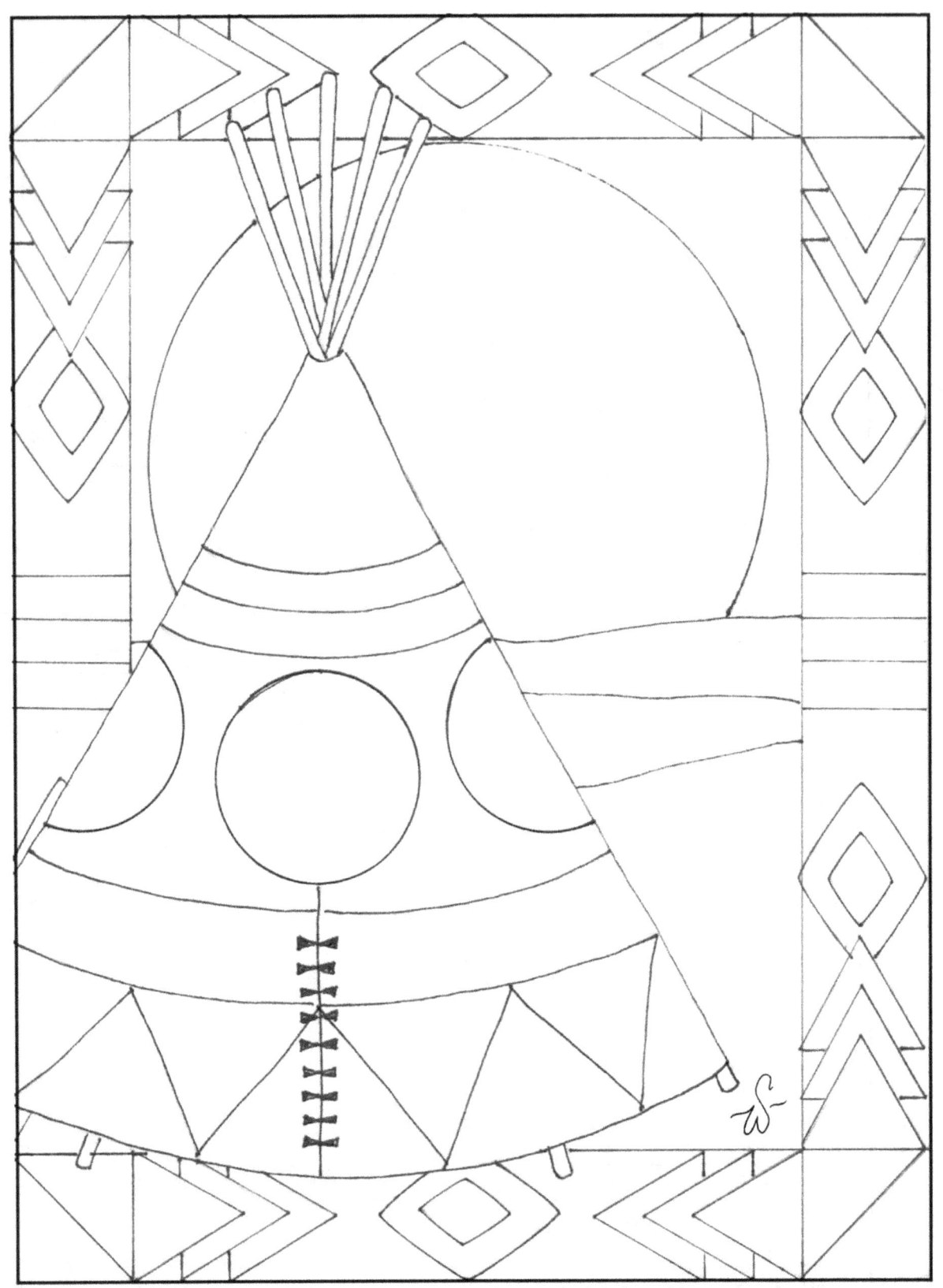

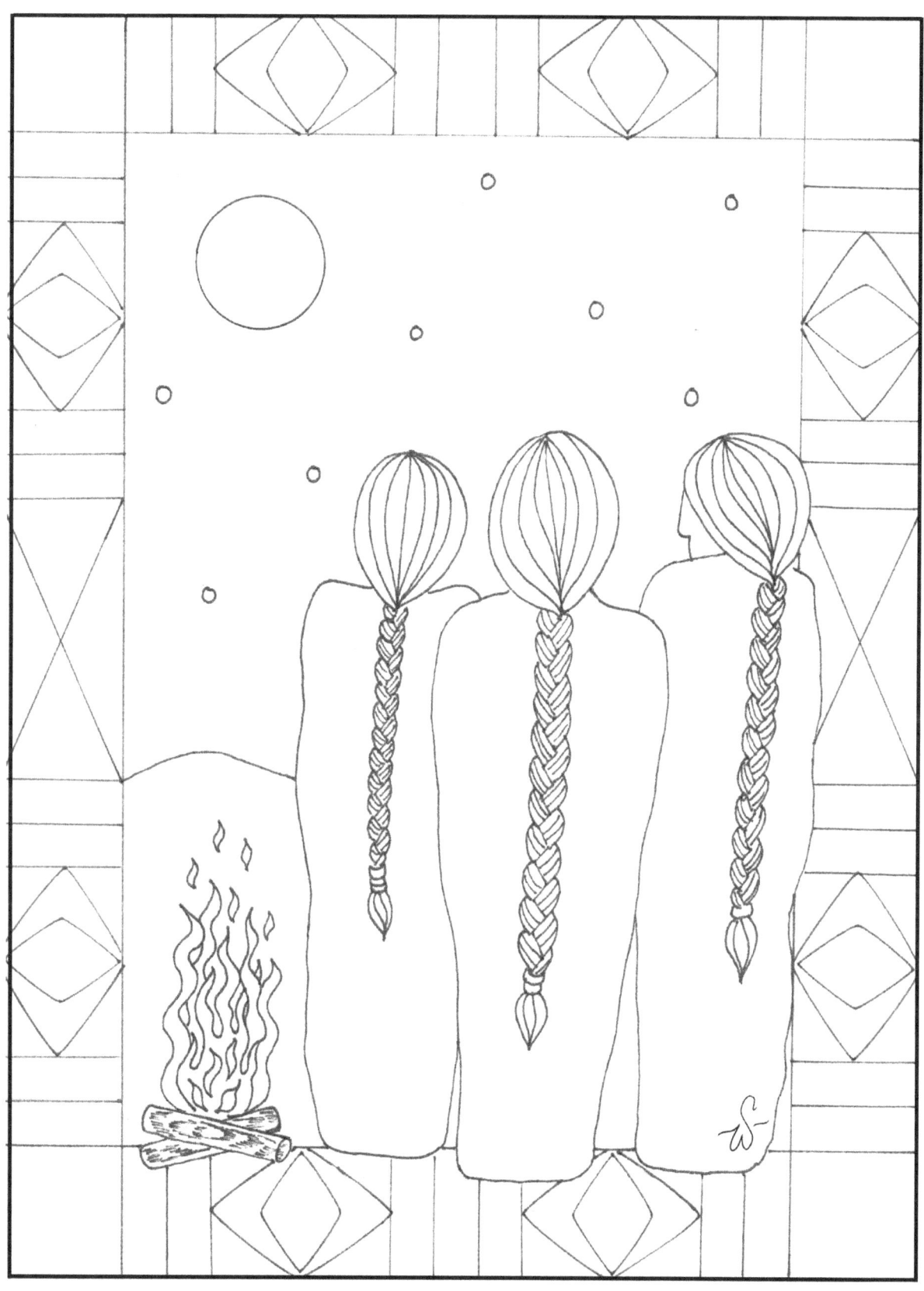

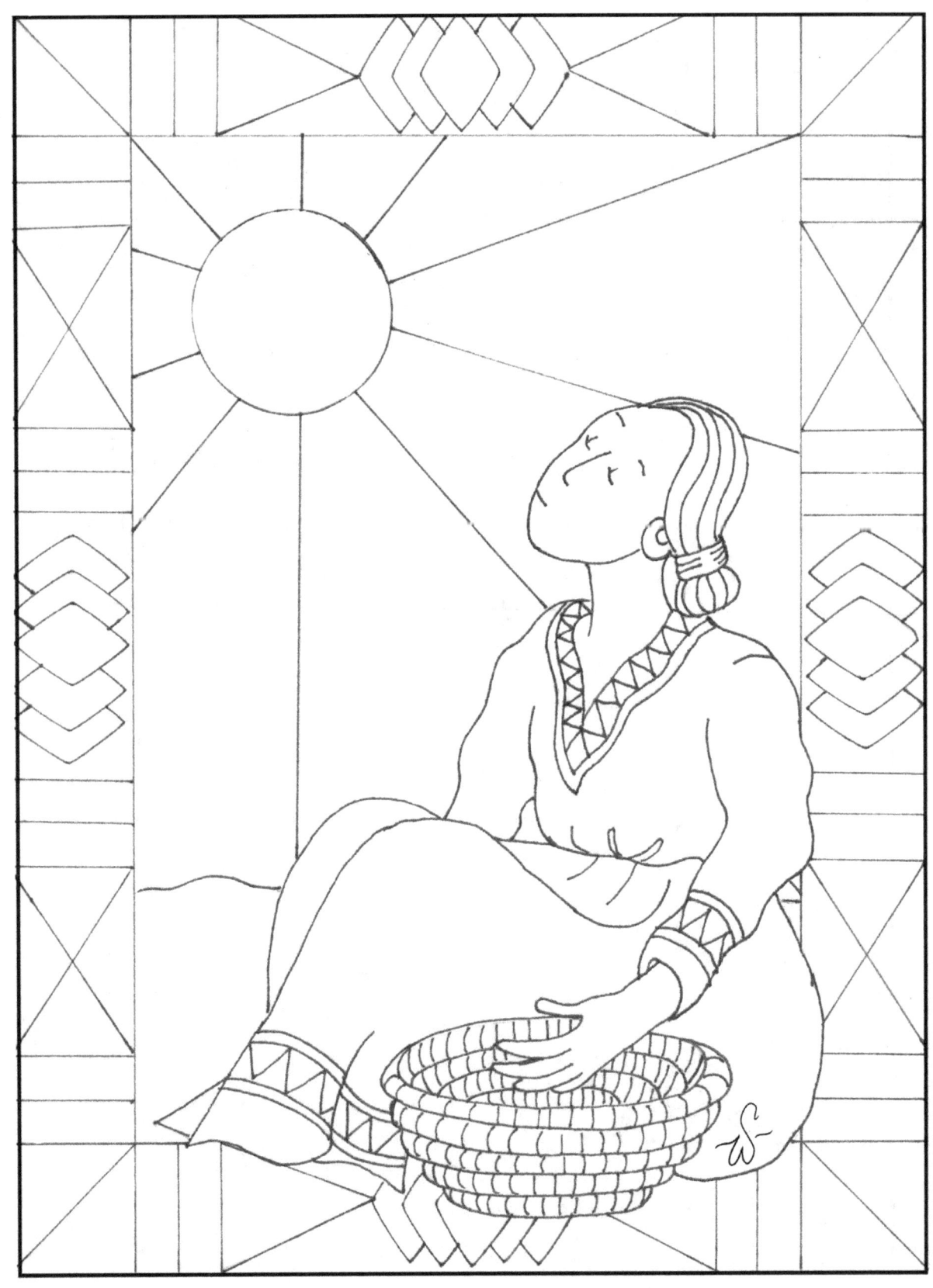

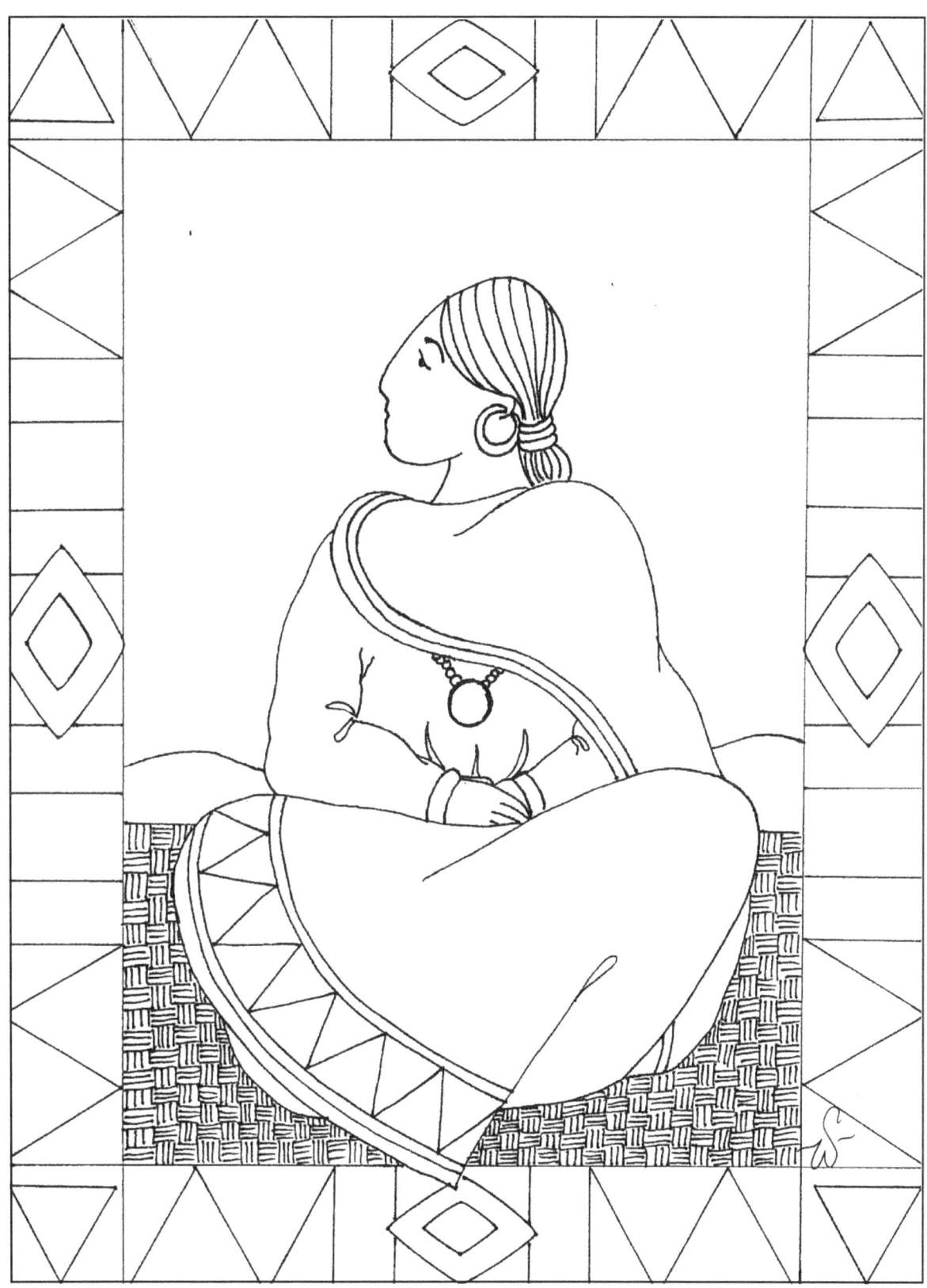

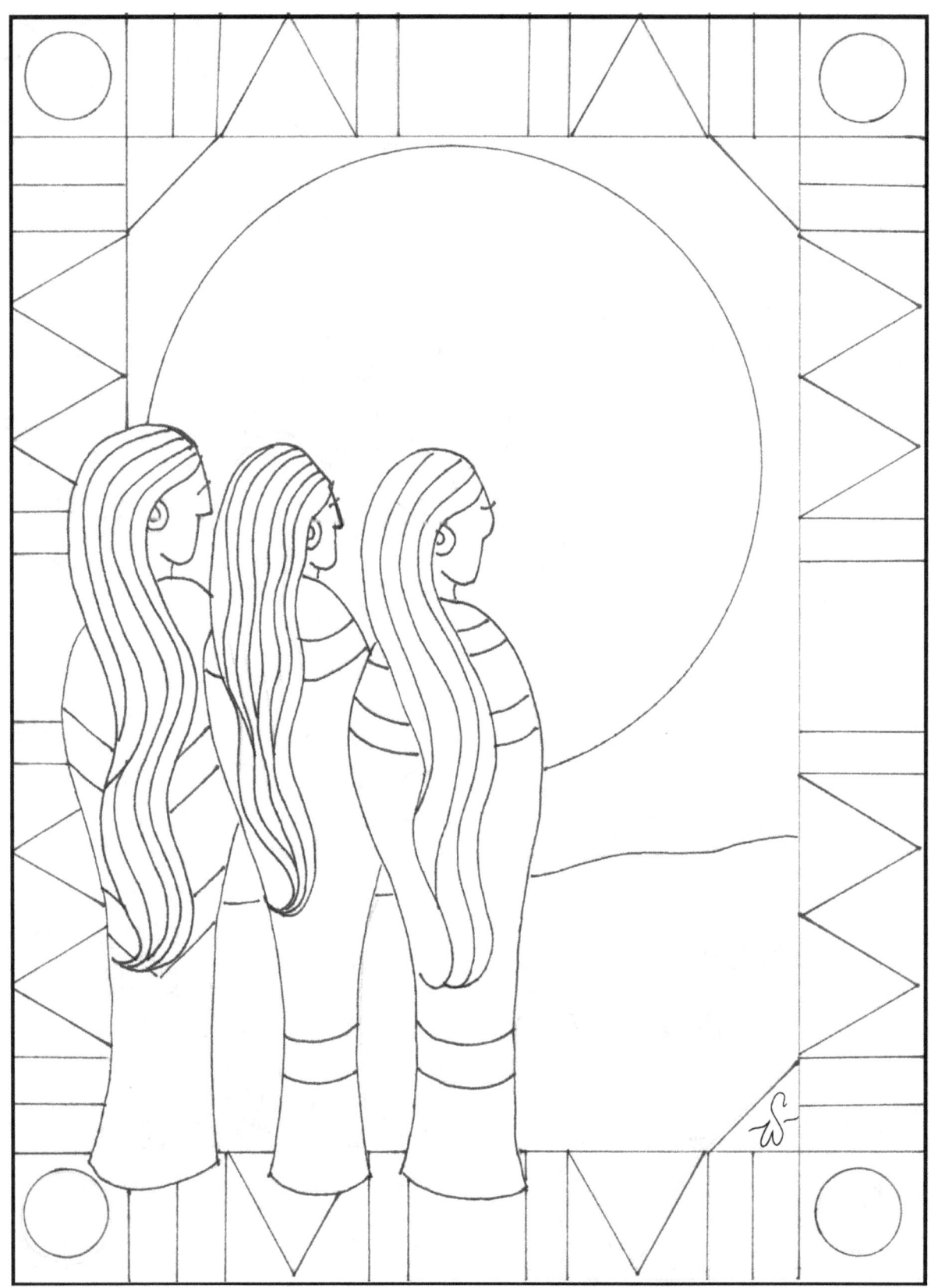

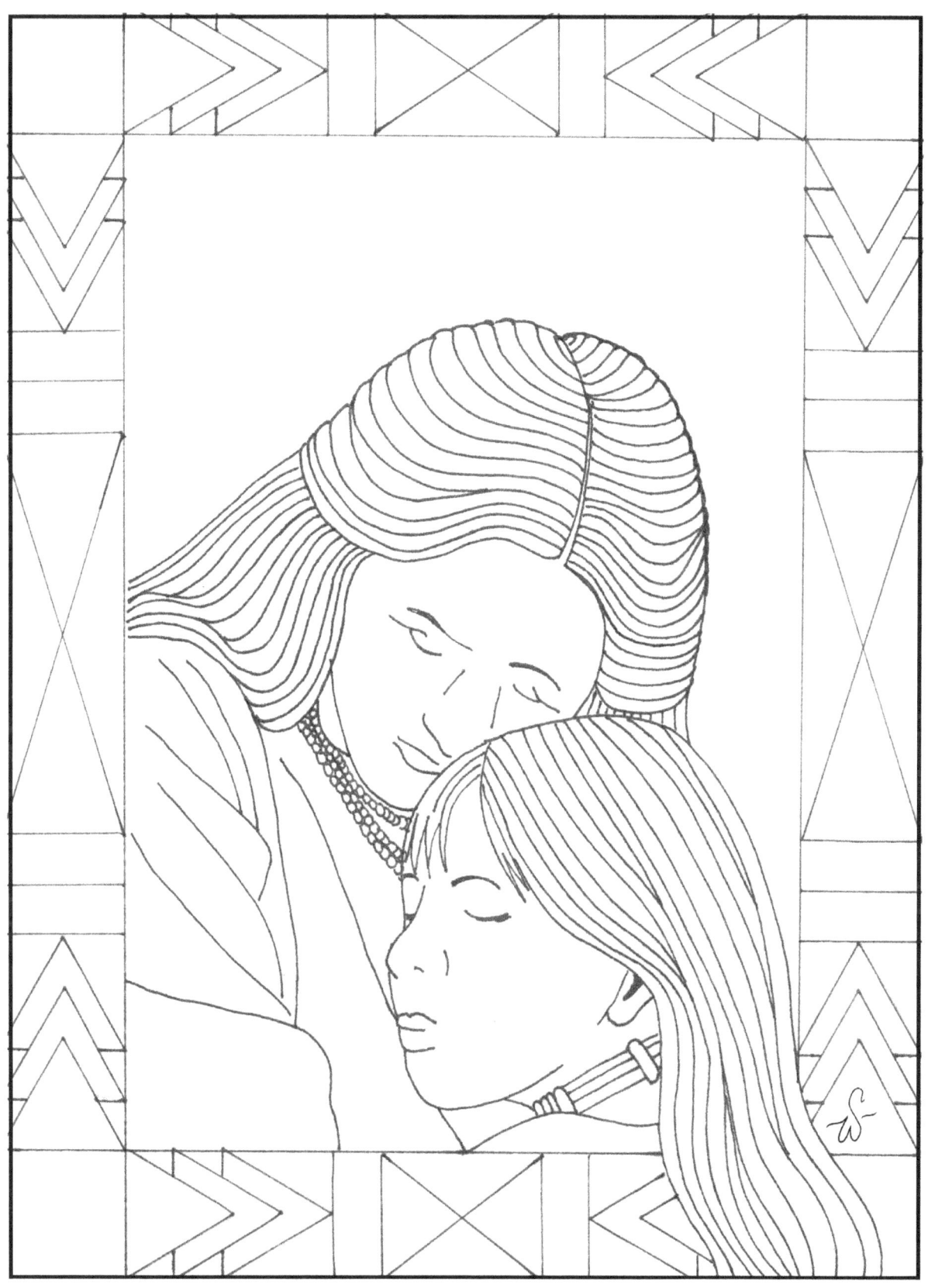

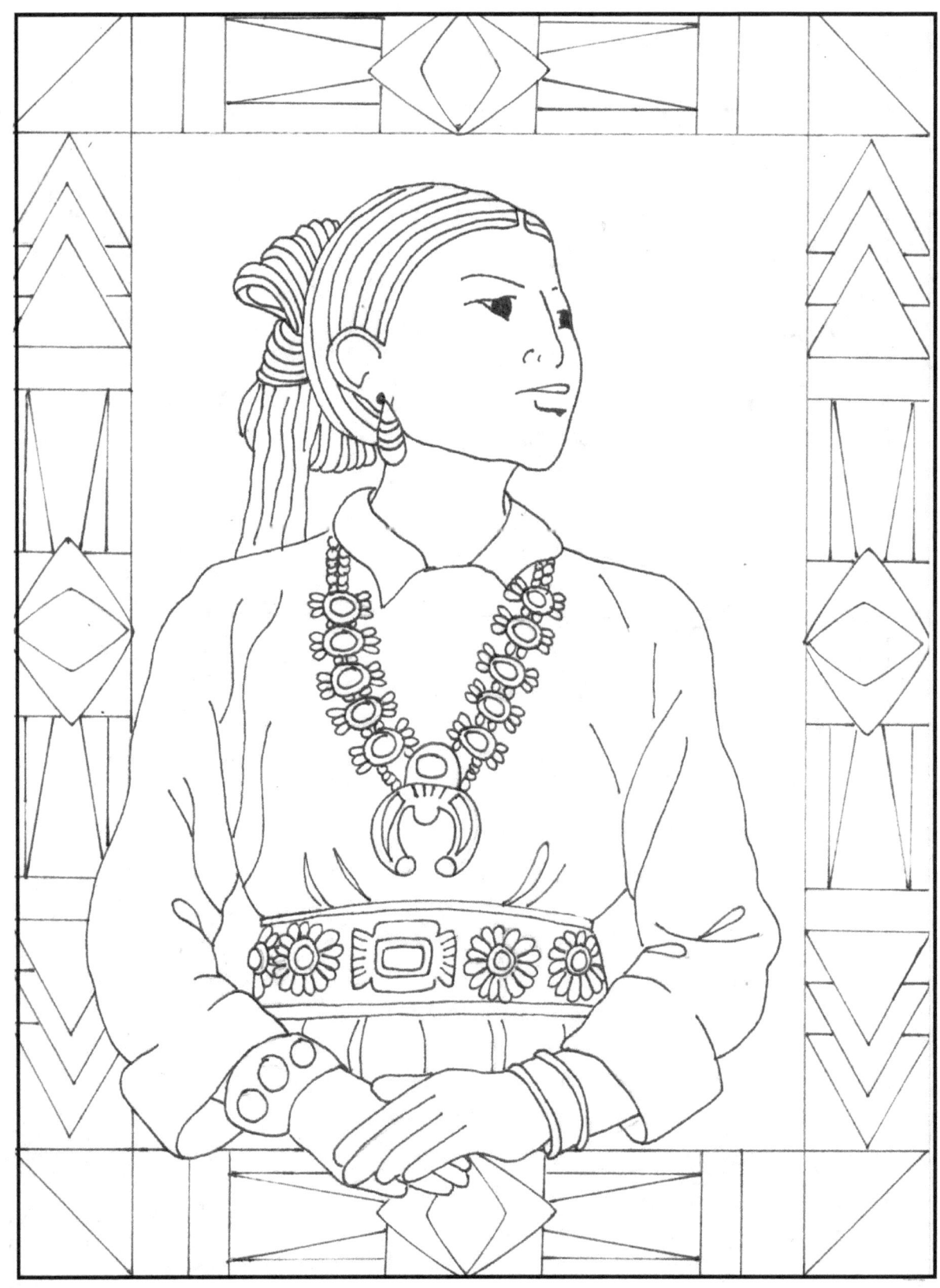

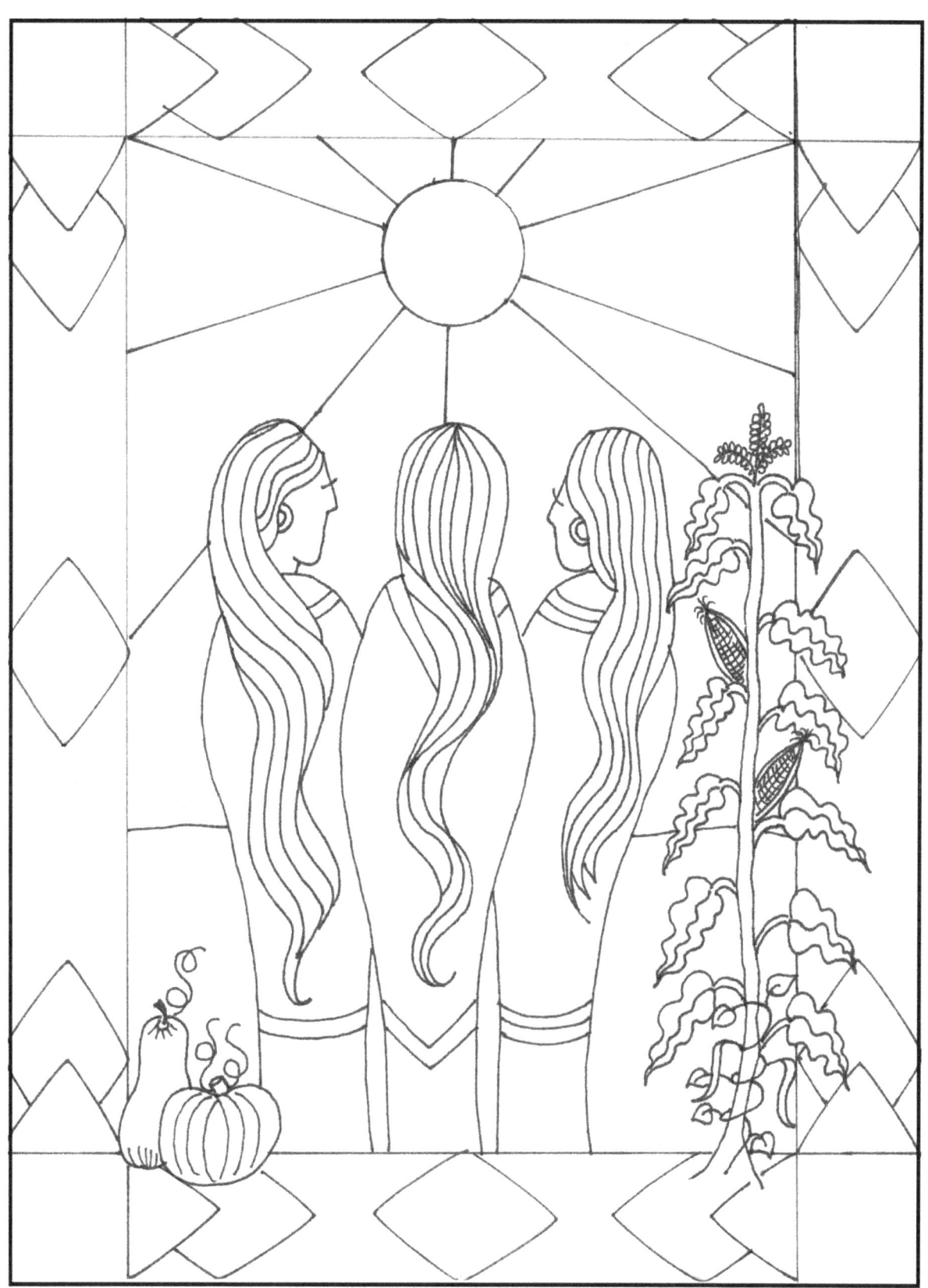

About the author:

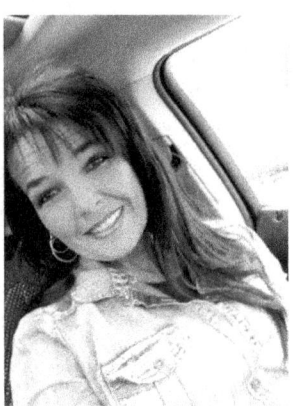

Weeya Michelle Smith has a BA in Art Education with a Masters in Technology Integration. Annually, she presents to elementary, middle and high schools in the Wisconsin area about Southeast Woodland People. She attends Living History Events and Rendezvous representing Southeast Woodland People as a storyteller and presenter in Wisconsin, Michigan, Illinois, & Indiana. Weeya is a certified Art teacher offering art classes and a motivational speaker to women, young & old, who have experienced trauma.

Weeya Michelle Smith is an enrolled citizen of the Echota Cherokee Tribe of Alabama. Being a citizen of a state recognized tribe, all her artwork is guaranteed to be "Native American Made" as she is covered under the Indian Arts and Crafts Act of 1990. This is a federal law which covers all federal and state recognized Native Americans. She is also a member of the Indian Arts and Crafts Association, which validates her work. The Alabama Indian Affairs Commission also backs her.

Thank you for purchasing Weeya Michelle Smith's first coloring book. Each drawing has become an original painting. To see the finished paintings and for more information, please visit her website at www.weeyasmith.com.

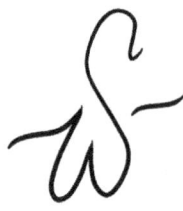